2007

I Sit and Stay

A Survival Guide for Kids (*and parents, too!*)

Get Sirius Press
Oakland, California

Written & Illustrated by Leah L. Waarvik

I Sit and Stay
A Survival Guide for Kids (and Parents, Too!)

Get Sirius Press
PO Box 13236
Oakland, CA 94661-9991
510-336-3604
www.GetSiriusPress.com
Book and cover design by Leah Waarvik and Michael Brechner

Emma

Koa

Disclaimer

Publisher's Cataloging-in Publication Data

Waarvik, Leah L.
   "I sit and stay": a survival guide for kids, and parents too! / Leah L. Waarvik. --
Oakland, Calif. : Get Sirius Press, 2007.
      p. ; cm.
   ISBN: 978-0-9797702-2-7

   Summary: Two search and rescue dogs help children learn wilderness survival skills. The author emphasizes the concept of "Sit and Stay" and what survival tools to carry and use when hiking or playing near the wilderness.

   1. Wilderness survival--Juvenile literature. 2. Survival skills--Juvenile literature. 3. Preparedness--Juvenile literature.
   4. [Survival.] I. Title. II. Survival guide for kids, and parents too.
   GV200.52 .W33 2007
   613.69--dc22 0709   2007932212

Printed in China
2 4 6 8 9 7 5 3 1

Foreword
To Parents and Teachers

Thank you for reading *I Sit and Stay: A Survival Guide for Kids (and Parents Too!)*. As Emma says on the first page, "You've taken the first step to making yourself and your child safer and smarter in the woods!" Now, before I talk about the book, let me introduce myself.

My name is Leah Waarvik. I'm a search-and-rescue professional. Emma is my K-9 partner. We're a certified wilderness search-and-rescue team with both CARDA (California Rescue Dog Association) and ALCOSAR (Alameda County Sheriff's Office Search-and-Rescue Team). I hold a National SAR Tech II certification and was a ground searcher with Alameda County before Emma and I joined their canine team. Both CARDA and ALCOSAR are highly respected organizations whose members have many years of search expertise and experience. I can proudly say that I drew on that knowledge to create this book and would not have been able to do so without my colleagues' input.

I decided to write *I Sit and Stay* after hearing stories of children who were lost and unprepared. I came to realize that the great presentations put on by search-and-rescue teams weren't reaching enough children. I think this is because people don't know about these resources, and because limited numbers of volunteers, who also hold full-time jobs, put on the presentations.

I wanted to create an option that was a bit more available and interactive for families that enjoy being outdoors. *I Sit and Stay* covers the basic principles of survival and is meant to initiate an interactive process between adults and children. It addresses the main points of survival, and I recommend that an adult supervise the hands-on portion that a presentation would usually cover — especially the garbage-bag portion! Children have been taught their whole lives not to put bags over their heads, and now two dogs in orange search vests are telling them that if they do this it can save their lives. Even though Emma recommends in the story that it's a good idea to do with a parent or teacher, it's up to you to explain that this is something to be done *only* when practicing with an adult or when you really are lost. For your own sanity you can also apply this rule to blowing the whistle.

Along with the garbage-bag drill you can do "lost in the woods" drills with your kids. Just like the fire department's suggestion that you practice fire drills in your home, I suggest you take your kids out and help them learn to evaluate a good "Sit-and-Stay" spot. Let them experiment with their garbage bags, play with their mirrors, and blow their whistles. I recommend doing this both in the daytime and at night. These drills will help children feel confident if ever they find themselves genuinely lost. As with anything involving children, the more exposure they have to something, the less scary it is.

Another thing I want to address is the "stranger" issue. Until very recently children were being taught "never talk to strangers." Organizations like the Polly Klaas Foundation[1] have moved away from this rigid teaching. The new method empowers kids to help them choose a safe person to help them. Unfortunately, in the woods or other remote locations, a lost child may not have many people to choose from. I deliberately decided not to use the "only go with a person in uniform" rule because civilians often become

part of a search effort — especially when there's a child involved. It's my opinion — and it's one shared by other search-and-rescue professionals — that children are in more danger from the elements and from injury outdoors than of being abducted by a stranger when they happen to be lost in the woods. There are many documented cases of children hiding from searchers. Here are two examples, fortunately with positive outcomes.

In June 2006, the *Rocky Mountain News* reported that Evan Thompson, who had wandered away from a Colorado campsite and was missing for four days, was finally found when he stopped to sit on a rock. Evan had been hiding from search helicopters because the noise scared him, and had hidden from searchers on the ground because he had been taught not to talk to strangers.

According to a June 2005 report from MSNBC News Service, Utah Boy Scout Scott Brennan's story is similar. After a four-day search, the missing boy was found standing in the middle of a trail. Scott had been hiding from searchers because he "didn't know if they were scary people."

If you're still hesitant about telling your children that they can talk to people they don't know when they're lost in the woods, let me offer you another option. You and your child can choose a "secret word" together. This is a word that's known only by your family and anyone that's involved in the outdoor activities your child participates in. If your child were to get lost, this secret word would be told to whoever is in charge of the search, and searchers would be directed to call

it out along with the child's name as they search. The secret word is a signal to the lost child that it's safe to come out. I speak for other rescuers and myself when I say that this isn't the best option because it teaches the child to hide, which, obviously, we don't want. There can also be periods of time when the search team isn't calling out, and they might just happen to be near your child at such a time.

The issue above is just one of the topics in the "More for Parents and Teachers" section at the end of this book. There's even more on my Web site, **www.ISitandStay.com**, where you can find links to other search-and-rescue resources. If you still have questions, I recommend consulting your local search-and-rescue group. They may do children's presentations, and will be helpful in answering your questions.

Enjoy the outdoors — and stay safe!
Leah Waarvik

Hi! I'm Emma and this is my friend Koa. We are certified wilderness search-and-rescue dogs, and we congratulate you for reading this survival guide! Whether you're a kid or all grown up, you've taken the first step to being safer and smarter in the woods! Now, before we start talking survival, let me tell you a bit about us.

POINT ISABEL

I first met Koa in my dog-training class, but this wasn't just *any* kind of dog training. We were in search-and-rescue-dog school.

In our class we learned how to use our noses to find children and grownups who are lost in the woods.

3

Koa and I are about the same age, but Koa had been in school longer than I had, so he already knew the ins and outs of search and rescue. He took me under his paw and showed me how to be a good student.

We worked
hard with our
handlers through lots of
training. After many tests we
finally graduated. Now that we're official
search dogs, we can teach you how to keep
yourself safe if you get lost in the woods. Your noses
aren't as good as ours, so we can't teach you how to smell
your way back home. But we can give you some tips that will
help us find you so you can get home safely.

SEARCH DOG

5

Lessons For The Week
Monday - Sit and Stay
Tuesday - Come when called
Wednesday - Heel
Thursday - No chasing cats! When they run from you it does NOT mean they want to be chased. This also goes for other small animals, cars, and the Mail carrier
Friday - No jumping on people (Especially Grandma!)

Let's start with one of the first things we learned: SIT and STAY! If you're lost, it's easier for us to find you if you sit, stay, and don't move from place to place.

This is Tabitha Trailtrotter.

Tabitha is smart because she has picked a place to Sit and Stay under a tree close to a trail.

This is a great place because it's right near the trail she was hiking on. Trails are some of the first places we search. The tree will also provide her some shelter from heat or cold while she waits to be found.

ROUNDNROUND ROAD

TRIKTYA TRAIL

KEEP BACK
300 FEET !

If I'm lost and can't find my way,
I Sit and Stay. I don't run away.
Emma and Koa are on their way.

Here's a rhyme that Tabitha uses to help
her remember these important rules.
It can help *you* too!

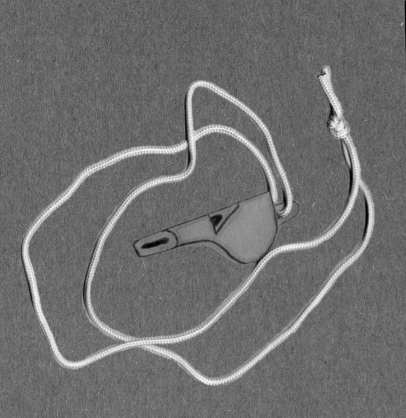

We'd also like to tell you about some things you should always carry. They can be a big help if you ever get lost outdoors.

A Whistle

A Garbage Bag

A Shiny Mirror

The most important thing is a loud whistle on a string. Always wear this whistle around your neck when you go hiking or camping with your friends or family. If you get lost, you should sit and stay in your Sit-and-Stay spot and blow the whistle as loud and as often as you can.

Our noses are the best, but Koa and I also use our ears to listen when we search. The people who help us are using their ears and eyes to find you as well. Our friend, Wendy Windpipe, has remembered to wear her whistle and is now blowing it over and over again while she waits for us to find her. This time it will be our ears instead of our noses that help us find Wendy.

Wendy also repeats the rhyme to help her remember what to do.

If I'm lost and can't find my way,
I Sit and Stay. I don't run away.
Emma and Koa are on their way.

Then she blows the whistle again.

Just like Wendy Windpipe, you can say the rhyme and blow the whistle over and over again while you wait for us to find you.

The other things that you should have with you are a garbage bag and a mirror. You should keep them in your pocket or pack where you always know where they are.

13

It sounds kind of silly, but a garbage bag can be a big help if you're lost. Benicio Bivouac is using his paw—oops, his finger—to make a big hole in his bag for his face. After he makes the hole big enough, he can wear the bag like a rain poncho. The poncho will keep him warm and dry until we find him.

Bivouac (biv-oo-wak): a temporary shelter or camp for sleeping in outside, not in the form of a tent.[2]

When we find you in your garbage-bag poncho, we'll try not to laugh. Remember: *Never* wear the garbage bag without first making the big hole. It's a good idea to make a bag with your parents or teacher before you're in the woods. Then you can test it out.

Can you remember the rhyme? Good job!

If you get lost, remember: Help is on the way. We have lots of search-and-rescue friends who will all be looking for you. They may look different from us, and you might not know them. You know that in most cases you shouldn't talk to people you don't know. But when you're lost in the woods the rules about talking to people you don't know are different.

F. FIXYAUP

MEDIC

C. COMETAFINDJA

K-9 RESCUE

If you see someone in the woods when you're lost, call out and ask for help. If the person can't hear your voice, blow your whistle. It will be louder than your voice. If you ever get lost in the woods, these friends you haven't met yet will help you find your way.

The people who will be looking for you may be calling your name loudly and blowing their whistles. These noises may sound scary at nighttime, or their voices may sound angry because they're yelling. But they aren't angry at all; they're just trying to find you. If you hear people yelling, you should yell back at them and blow your whistle. This will help them find you.

There are other noises in the woods that may sound scary, too. Animals in the woods don't want to hurt you. They're actually afraid of you! If you hear a strange noise, you can yell and blow your whistle. If the noise you heard was an animal, it will get scared and run away. If the noise is from one of our friends, they'll come and help you.

If you feel scared, try saying the rhyme out loud.

If I'm lost and can't find my way,
I Sit and Stay. I don't run away.
Emma and Koa are on their way.

If you still feel scared after saying the rhyme, just think of yourself wearing that garbage bag. That will make you laugh!

Some of our friends may also come in airplanes or helicopters to help find you. Helicopters and planes are sometimes loud and you might think they sound scary, but helicopters and planes are important search tools. The pilot and copilot have a great view of open spaces from the air. An open space is an area that doesn't have a lot of trees or bushes. These open spaces are great places to use the third item that you have with you—the mirror.

Ryan Reflecto has picked a great place to Sit and Stay. It's next to a tree near a big open space so he can be seen from a helicopter or a plane.

He knows that if he sees a plane or a helicopter, he should try to make himself look big so he's easier to see. This is where the shiny mirror comes in. You can see that Ryan is using his shiny mirror to reflect the sun toward the helicopter so the pilot can see him.

Ryan Reflecto has also used sticks and rocks to make a big arrow in the open space, pointing to his Sit-and-Stay spot. He knows that it's okay to get up from his Sit-and-Stay spot to make signs or to make himself look big in the open space as the helicopter passes. Ryan makes sure his Sit-and-Stay spot is always in sight, and he always goes back to it when he's done.

Our super-smart friends have shown you some great Sit-and-Stay spots. They know that these Sit-and-Stay spots may have to change a bit if it starts to thunder and lightning. Wendy Windpipe and Ryan Reflecto remember that lightning likes to strike the tallest thing around, so they'll pick their new spots wisely.

Wendy Windpipe has found a group of small trees not far from her original Sit-and-Stay spot. She knows the trees will be safer because they're closer to the ground than the tall tree she was near.

Ryan Reflecto has chosen a small tree that's farther away from the open space. He'll crouch there until the storm ends. He knows that helicopters and planes won't be flying until the storm has passed, so he'll wait until it's over and then return to his spot in the open space.

If Ryan were in an open space with no trees at all he would go to the lowest part of it and crouch down. If there was a low rock to crouch on, that would be a great place, too.

Now, we've told you many things that will help you if you're lost, but we think the best thing ever would be if we never even had to look for lost children. We'd much rather spend our days at the dog park or hiking on trails. So remember: always stay with an adult or in sight of people when you go camping or hiking in the woods.

Always carry your three special items:

A Whistle

A Garbage Bag

A Shiny Mirror

Be aware! Stay on trails, don't take shortcuts, and try to keep your campsite or car within sight.

If I'm lost and can't find my way,
I Sit and Stay. I don't run away.
Emma and Koa are on their way.

Smelly People are the Best People!

But if you do get lost or turned around, remember the rhyme.
And remember to **Sit** and **Stay!**

More for Parents And Teachers

After reading the book, you know a little more about how to keep you and your child safe. I hope you've also read the foreword, played with the whistle, the garbage bag, and the mirror, and have even done some "lost in the woods" drills. The kids' portion touches on the main points that I wanted to get across to children, but a picture book has its limitations. This is where I need your help to expand on some issues that I touched upon in the story.

Lost (adj.): Strayed or missing [3]

Let's start with the concept of being lost. This is sometimes a hard one for kids, especially little ones. It's hard to say at what age kids really get this concept, so the best we can do is come up with some creative ways to talk about it. Here are some suggestions.

You may be lost when you've been playing or hiking and you suddenly realize you're by yourself. A friend may be with you, but you can't see your parent or teacher. You call out for someone and they don't answer, you blow your whistle and no one comes right away. This is when you "Sit and Stay!"

You don't have to be scared when you're lost. In fact try to teach your children that there's no reason to be afraid when they're lost because they're prepared and they know what to do. Experts say that "PMA" (positive mental attitude) is the first key to survival [4] and is in fact just as important as the three special items.

🐾 Teach them how to improvise if they happen to have forgotten their three special items. If they don't have them, they can still "Sit and Stay."

🐾 Explain the importance of being aware in unfamiliar surroundings. While you do want kids to be kids, it's important for them to get in the habit of checking in with you on a hike or in the campground.

🐾 The Buddy System is a good technique if you have more than one child.

The Garbage Bag

As I mentioned in the foreword, the most obvious danger of the garbage bag is suffocation. Although the bag is big, there's still a risk. Stress the importance of making the hole along with the fact that the bag should be used only in drills that are supervised and when the child is really lost. Another risk is overheating. The child should wear the bag when it's cold and/or raining, but *not* in the hot sun.

The Whistle

The whistle is a safety tool. It should be blown *only* when someone needs help!

The Mirror

I've included instructions and a diagram on how to use the mirror on pages 34 and 35.

Sit and Stay Spots

Emma does a good job of describing good "Sit-and-Stay" spots, but here's some more information for you.

- If your child chooses a "Sit-and-Stay" spot near a trail, he or she will be easier to find. The first phase of a search is usually a "hasty search" in which we go down the trails calling out the lost person's name.

- If your child chooses a "Sit-and-Stay" spot near a trail that's near an open space, this is even better. Here the child has the possibility of being found by ground teams or air teams.

- The essential thing I want to get across is that if children can see a good "Sit-and-Stay" spot from where they realize they're lost, it's okay for them to walk to that spot. We just don't want them wandering around looking for the perfect spot while unknowingly getting farther from the last place you saw them. As I said in the foreword, it's a good exercise to go out and evaluate good "Sit-and-Stay" spots together. Talk about why you would or wouldn't choose certain ones.

Be Prepared

The better you and your child are prepared as a team, the better the chances are for finding you or your child quickly. Here are some recommendations for being prepared.

1. Have a meeting place out of the woods. Okay, now you're confused: the child should be "Sitting and Staying," right? Yes, but if a "friend they hadn't met yet" has helped your child out of the woods, the child should know where to meet you. Hopefully the Good Samaritan has brought your child out of the woods directly into your loving arms, but if not, the child should be able to tell this helpful person where your "meeting place" is, or at least describe it.

2. Know where resources are. Things to note would be ranger stations, telephones, populated areas, etc. Note these things if you're coming to an unfamiliar area. If you're in a park there's a good chance you won't have cellular reception, so have a backup plan to get help if you need to. If you would need to leave the parking lot to get help, work this into your "meeting plan." Let your child know that if your car is gone from the "meeting place" you've gone to get help and he or she should stay there until you return.

3. Take note of the clothes your child is wearing before you leave for your outing. This information can be extremely helpful to searchers, as it's very common for children to drop clothing if they're lost. Teach your children that it's a good idea to keep their extra clothing just in case. In the book Emma tells them "keep your special items in your pocket or pack." My preference would be their pockets—kids are kids and they lose things. The pack is a backup in case they don't have pockets.

4. Get help as soon as you can. Here are some steps you can take if you realize you don't know where your child is. You can improvise with different scenarios.

- 🐾 Don't panic, remember "PMA" (positive mental attitude).[5] Think back and remember the last place that you saw her.

- 🐾 Go to the place you last saw the child and call out. Remember to call out and then *listen*. If the child doesn't answer, use the same technique blowing your whistle.

- 🐾 Go to your "meeting place." If you can call for help from the meeting place, do it now while you wait for the child to show up.

- 🐾 If you can't call for help from the meeting place, ask someone to call for help while you wait. Give them specific instructions to call for help and then come back to tell you that they've reached someone.

- 🐾 If you can't call for help from the meeting place and there's no one around to help you, use your own judgment. In a remote area you may decide to wait for an hour for someone to show up. If no one does, go for help yourself. Remember that your child knows that if your car is gone from the meeting place, you've gone to get help and he or she knows to wait for you there

5. **If you get separated from your child, try to remember the last place you saw him.** If you can, mark the place with whatever you can. Also mark the location on a map if you have one.

6. **Keep a recent picture of your child with you.** Many parents keep photos of their kids in purses or wallets, but if you're like me you might not take all of those things hiking. Just in case, keep an extra picture in the glove box of your car. It's also not a bad idea to leave an itinerary on the front seat or dashboard. Note the day and time and where you planned to hike, so if *you* get lost, we'll know where to start searching for you.

Friends You Haven't Met Yet

The days of telling kids "never talk to strangers" are gone. The new phrase is "Keep Your Kids Safe, Not Scared."[6] You can find out more about how to keep your kids safe at **www.pollyklaas. org.** They offer child-safety kits, which include DNA and fingerprinting kits, and more information about how to talk to your kids about this sensitive issue.

Recyclable Footprints

To most of us a picture is worth 1,000 words, but to the highly skilled individuals called trackers a picture of a footprint is worth many more. Each person's shoes, step, and stride are different. Believe it or not, a tracker can follow these marks through the wilderness to help locate a lost person. You can create a footprint picture for a tracker using a simple piece of aluminum foil. Just put the foil on the ground and step on it. When you're done, put it in a book or magazine. This picture saves the trackers the time of eliminating all the similar tracks that belong to other people. This is a fun exercise for kids, and at the end of the trip you can teach them the importance of recycling by throwing their footprints into the recycle bin.

Frequently Asked Questions

1: Should my child carry water on a hike? I've heard that water is important, so why isn't it one of the "Special Items?"

Answer: Yes, your child should carry water on a hike. Water is very important. It's not one of the "Special Items" because it's not as important as shelter (the garbage bag). In survival there's something we call the "Rule of Fours." It goes like this:

You can survive

4 minutes without air;

4 hours without shelter;

4 days without water;

4 weeks without food.

If the other recommendations are followed, the odds of a lost person being found within four days increase. Nearly all survival situations today are short term (72 hours or less). The much-publicized long-term survival experiences make up fewer than 5 percent of all incidents.[7]

It's great if you can get your children to carry water in a backpack or fanny pack, but it's better if they keep their "Special Items" in their pockets. They're more likely to lose a backpack or fanny pack than to lose their pants.

2: What should I carry when I go hiking?

Answer: Your three special items, of course! At the very minimum, you should also carry water, a first-aid kit, a trail map (if you know how to read one), and your cell phone. You would add to this list depending on the length of the outing you plan. Some other things to add would be extra clothing, rain gear, snacks, and water-purification tablets.

3: What's the best kind of clothing to wear when hiking?

Answer: You may have heard the saying "cotton kills." The best materials for hiking are synthetic. There are many versions these days, but mainly you're looking for a material that "wicks" moisture away and dries quickly. If you or your child is stuck outside, the worst thing to be is cold and wet. If your clothes are wet, it's actually better to be in your garbage bag without them on than to stay in them and be cold. Bright colors are also a bonus when we're trying to find a lost person.

Instructions for Using The Signal Mirror

On the page to the right there's a diagram showing how to aim the signal mirror.

Imagine the hands in the picture are your hands. One hand is giving the "Thumbs-up" sign. The other hand is holding the signal mirror with the shiny side facing toward the sun.

Identify your target and place your thumb over it. (In the diagram the target is the helicopter window).

Holding the "Thumbs-up" hand still, move the mirror to shine the sun's reflection onto your thumb.

Once you've aimed the reflection, you can move your thumb so the sun can shine on your target.

Using a signal mirror takes practice. It's a good idea to practice with your parents or teacher. When you're practicing you can use tall trees or tall buildings as targets. You should *never* shine the mirror into anyone's eyes, or at cars, planes, or helicopters when you are not lost.

If you've lost or forgotten your mirror you can use other shiny items to signal! Some good ones are pieces of foil, CDs, shiny metal cans, and watches.

Notes

1. The Polly Klaas Foundation: **www.pollyklaas.org**

2. **http://dictionary.cambridge.org**

3. *American Heritage College Dictionary*, 2nd ed.

4. *Search and Rescue Fundamentals-Basic Skills and Knowledge to Perform Wilderness, Inland, Search and Rescue*, Cooper, LaValla and Stoffel, 3rd ed., revised.

5. *Search and Rescue Fundamentals-Basic Skills and Knowledge to Perform Wilderness, Inland, Search and Rescue*, Cooper, LaValla and Stoffel, 3rd ed., revised.

6. The Polly Klaas Foundation: **www.pollyklaas.org**

7. *Search and Rescue Fundamentals-Basic Skills and Knowledge to Perform Wilderness, Inland, Search and Rescue.* Cooper, LaValla and Stoffel, 3rd ed., revised.

Emma's and Koa's
Dog-Park Pals

Oliver

Annie